Touchable God:
Finding the Lord's Friendship Through Prayer

Jeanette Levellie

© 2016 Jeanette Levellie

ISBN: 978-1-365-26177-0

"Baby Princess" was originally published in *Life Lessons from Moms,* compiled by Suzanne Williams and Tracy Ruckman (Write Integrity Press, 2012).

"A Jolly Miracle" was originally published in *The Exraordiary Presence of God,* compiled and edited by Ann White Knowles (Pix-N-Pens Publishing, 2015).

"Little People" was originally published in *Faith and Friends* magazine, Ken Ramstead, editor

Unless otherwise noted, all Scriptures are taken from the Holy Bible, New International Version®, NIV®. Copyright © 1973, 1978, 1984, 2011 by Biblica, Inc.™ Used by permission of Zondervan. All rights reserved worldwide. www.zondervan.com

Scripture references marked AMP are taken from the Amplified® Bible, Copyright © 2015 by The Lockman Foundation. Used by permission. www.Lockman.org

Scripture references marked NASB are taken from the New American Standard Bible®, Copyright © 1960, 1962, 1963, 1968, 1971, 1972, 1973, 1975, 1977, 1995 by The Lockman Foundation. Used by permission. www.Lockman.org.

Scripture references marked NKJV are taken from the New King James Version, Copyright © 1982 by Thomas Nelson, Inc. Used by permission. All rights reserved.

PRAISE for *Touchable God:*

"I have been teaching and writing on prayer for over 20 years and have found that telling stories of answered prayer and teaching about prayer as relationship is the most effective way to encourage and stretch the prayer lives of others! Jeanette Levellie's new book, *Touchable God: Finding the Lord's Friendship through Prayer,* is remarkable for several reasons. First, she breaks the barriers of religiosity and shares the freedom and creativity to relate to God as our personal, compassionate, loving friend. God is approachable, and He is powerful! Second, you will see how simple it is to carry on an ongoing dialog with the Father about your life and the lives and situations of others. You will be blessed by her personal, engaging stories as you also gain confidence to speak to and hear from our Touchable God!"
-- **Kim Butts**, co-founder of Harvest Prayer Ministries, author, teacher and seeker of new, creative ways to engage with God!

"Jeanette Levellie's *Touchable God* charms, inspires, and moves the reader to believe in a God who is not distant but close, not indifferent but involved, and not illusory but immanent. The relatable stories and prayers drawn from her own life and the honest, vulnerable way she writes will make you laugh, cry, and draw closer to a God who is always drawing closer to you."
--**Bob Hostettler,** of *Red Letter Life* and T*he Bard and the Bible (A Shakespeare Devotional)*

"Jeanette brings years of experience as a dedicated person of prayer, as well as finely-developed writing skills, to a subject which is, while somewhat mysterious, central to Christian faith and practice."
--**Rev. Rodger Allen,** co-pastor, The Presbyterian Church, Paris, IL

"In the midst of personal crisis, words sometimes fail me or I get confused. I want to pray   but have no idea what to say or if I can really say *that* to God. When a loved one is facing a horrible disease or painful loss, I want to offer them a compassionate response, but not say the wrong thing. *Touchable God*, by Jeanette Levellie, contains composed prayers that address most all of my needs. Her words have helped me express my hearts longings to God, and helped me more boldly intercede for others. I highly recommend this book."
--Diana L. Flegal, Literary Agent/Blogger/ Adventurer

"Jeanette Levellie is best known for her wonderful sense of humor, but in this book, she reveals a holy sense of wonder through warm and witty stories of a *Touchable God*.
-- **James N. Watkins**, award-winning author and speaker

"Jeanette Levellie touches us where we live, giving glimpses into our past by sharing hers. She knows her heart and opens it freely for us. We can see with her, feel with her, love with her, and pray with her. *Touchable God* answers many questions women have but are too afraid or too busy to ask. We can now whisper (or read) a prayer in the morning, afternoon, and evening, thanks to Jeanette."
--Debbie Hardy, Queen of Resilience & Author of *Free to Be Fabulous*

"Jeanette Levellie has a way of taking a complex topic and simplifying it with a dash of humor. She does so from a peer-to-peer level rather than a student-teacher position. You'll laugh with her, cry with her and nod your head as she shares relatable experiences from her life in *Touchable God*.
-- **Susan J. Reinhardt**, Author of *The Moses Trilogy* and *The Christmas Wish*

"Jeanette Levellie's classic, heartfelt warmth shines through in her latest book, *Touchable God*. The combination of true, insightful stories and uplifting prayers offers light and wisdom, illustrating God's approachable and loving nature. This book is a wonderful, poignant lifeline of encouragement and hope to hearts of all ages.
--Karen Lange, freelance writer, editor, and author

"What I love about *Touchable God* is that Jeanette Levellie shares down-to-earth stories that are easy to relate to—each story as special and unique as each of us is in God's eyes. Jeanette focuses on our relationship with God and He how longs for us, rather than writing out a long list of 'thou shalt' and 'thou shalt not' items that would make anyone feel discouraged. Her prayers are based on Scripture, yet speak to us today in the 21st century, spotlighting the challenges that we face in today's hurried and hectic times, reminding us that God offers us the same rest in Him that he offered to prophets long ago. I encourage you to read *Touchable God*. When you do, prepare to go on a joyful journey with Jeanette, as her love of our Lord resonates in every syllable."
--**Kelly Boyer-Sagert,** author of *Everything to God in Prayer: A Writer's Weekly Devotional*

"With a passion for people, a heart filled with love, a wit overflowing with humor, and a desire for people to see Jesus, Jeanette Levellie is active in the lives of her audience. You'll love her as a friend and trust her as a confidant as she communicates God's truth, love, and humor in practical ways."
---**Elaine W. Miller**, Author/Speaker,
www.SplashesofSerenity.com

"Jeanette combines wisdom and gentle humor to mend tattered souls. Her sweet spirit and selfless attitude rest upon her listeners like a nurse's reassuring hand. She is one of the most compassionate, encouraging Christians you will ever meet."
--- **Cammie Quinn**, Author

Table of Contents

Dedicated to

my mom, Doris Kidgell,

a sterling example

of prayer,

&

all my prayer partners throughout the years:

Kevin Levellie, Kathy Nobilione, Bev Mathieson,

Nancy Sanchez, Carol Drey, Deborah McClarey,

Diana Savage, Beth Gormong, Dee Stark,

Cecelia Lester, James N. Watkins,

Karen Lange, Cammie Quinn, and Diana Flegal.

Your love has made me strong.

Acknowledgments

Author, magazine editor, and conference director Lin Johnson says, "Be prepared to be tested on whatever you write." *Aha.* Perhaps that's why I was tested in my walk with the Lord throughout the writing of *Touchable God.* But, as you can see, Jesus triumphed once again.

He always does.

Thanks to many lovely friends and the Holy Spirit for your encouragement and help these last few years:

Kevin, for being my anchor, advisor, and answer man,

Marie, Ron, Jenessa, Daniel, and Grace, for constant inspiration to keep going,

Diana Flegal, for believing in this project even when I didn't,

Dee Stark and Beth Gormong, for praying me through the storms,

Diana Savage, for helping me feel like a spiritual Navy SEAL when I felt like Gomer Pyle, and for your brilliant editing help,

Betty Kelly, for smiling in the dark and for inspiring the title, *Touchable God.*

Section I
My Journey with Jesus

Touching God has not come easily for me. Because I grew up in an alcoholic home, my view of God as my Father was a contrast between overindulgence and unreasonable demands. The road to seeing God as perfect love that casts out fear was a rocky, winding one. And I still trip over religious rocks and fall into puddles of past regrets. Just not as often as before.

As you read these stories of how God showed me His touchable nature, I hope you'll be encouraged to believe that you also can experience an intimate, moment-by-moment relationship with the Lord, where you talk openly with your Father and hear from Him.

My prayer for you is that you get a glimpse—no, make that a huge, panoramic view—of the bottomless heart of a faithful God, and dare to believe and ask for more than you've ever imagined. May *Touchable God* lead you from a joyless religion into a joy-filled relationship with the Lord.

These stories are for you.

1. Rodger Opened One Eye!

When my husband, Kevin, and I were newlyweds, a friend in the small church we pastored helped me get a job teaching music at a Catholic school. I knew little about teaching or music, but I was taking piano lessons, so perhaps they saw some potential in me. Either that or they were desperate to fill the position when the lady they'd hired never returned from a trip to visit her sick mother.

I was in the first-grade classroom one day when a siren interrupted my lesson. All the children stood up, clasped their hands, bowed their heads, and recited the Hail Mary prayer. I stood with my eyes closed out of respect for their practice. When the prayer was finished, six-year-old Mike spouted, "Why didn't you pray, teacher?"

"I did pray. I asked God to help whoever was in an accident."

"But that's not right," he said.

Paul was quick to argue with Mike. "Yes it is! My dad says you can pray however you want. So when I get up in the morning, I say, 'Howdy, God. How ya doin'?'"

Whew. Was I ever grateful to Paul's father that day. Not simply because his instruction helped me out of an uncomfortable moment, but also because he taught his son that he could talk to the Lord as a friend. Although Paul may have continued to say the memorized prayers he'd learned in church, he was on the road to a genuine relationship with God as a friend.

I wish I'd known that at age six.

My first memories of praying are from Sunday school and vacation Bible school. While we gathered around a kid-sized table—usually painted a garish green or obnoxious orange—the teacher would say, "Now, boys and girls, fold your hands, bow your heads, and close your eyes so we can thank God for our cookies and punch."

After the "amen," one of the boys would invariably tattle on another for breaking a rule. "Rodger had one eye open, teacher!"

The teacher would then say, "How did you know unless your eyes were open, Charlie?"

I understand the reasoning behind closed eyes, clasped hands, and bowed heads for youngsters. It keeps them from hitting each other or sneaking a cookie while the teacher prays. It may also aid in training them to concentrate while talking to the Lord.

But I carried the *proper prayer posture* rules into adulthood, thinking I had not prayed correctly unless I was kneeling with hands clasped and eyes closed. I was twenty-five before I realized that I could talk to my heavenly Father while pulling weeds, pacing around an empty church building, or feeding my baby in the middle of the night.

As a young desperate pastor's wife, I longed to see spiritual growth in the congregation we led. A friend suggested I go over to the church building twenty yards from our house and pray for our parishioners while walking the aisles. I'd leave my two young children with my husband Kevin for an hour or so and pace the church while praying. At first, I felt silly and awkward. But the more I talked to the Lord while walking, the easier it became. I realized that God is wherever I am, since His Holy Spirit lives in me.

This led me to try praying in other positions. While driving (I keep both eyes open!), while cooking and cleaning, and even in the shower.

I now realize that God is a person Who wants a relationship with me even more than I want to know Him. He doesn't care what position I'm in when I pray, as long as I let Him in on my life so He can help me live it. I've found I can't do life alone. I need Him every second.

Even more than I need cookies and punch.

2. Baby Princess

When I helped Mom clean out a closet the year I turned twelve, the photo of a gleeful toddler clutching a miniature scepter fascinated me. So did Mom's explanation of it.

"That's when you won first prize in the church's baby contest. Pastor Ben always called you *Princess* after that." *Oh, yes. The silver-haired, lanky pastor scooping me into his arms had sweetened every Sunday morning of my first six years.* What fun to discover the origin of his title for me.

As a child, I'd occupied myself with hopscotch, cartoons, and paper dolls. I never thought about my looks. Upon nearing my teens, I became obsessed with the length of my eyelashes, the frizz of my hair, and the size of my jeans. If I'd won a Beautiful Baby contest—even ten years before—perhaps there was hope for what my future mirror would say. But Mom's next words crumpled that dream.

"I always thought the judges gave you the prize because they felt sorry for you."

In spite of my wounded pride, curiosity reigned. "Why did they feel sorry for me?"

"Because you'd been very sick and had just come out of the hospital. We'd been worried you might die."

I stared in shock at the picture of the chubby-cheeked toddler. "You're kidding. I look perfectly healthy here. "

Mom's eyes misted over as she nodded. "You were healthy by that time. Everyone in the church had been praying for you, and God gave us a miracle."

Now I had to know the entire story. I handed the photo to Mom and plopped down on the carpet. "What was wrong with me?"

"Well, from the time you were born, you were always pale and pasty-looking. We didn't worry much about it. Since you were a redhead, we just thought you were fair-skinned. Then, at your eighteen-month checkup, the doctor became concerned because he thought you were too pale, even for a redhead." Her voice wobbled. "He suspected leukemia."

She gazed at the photo, now a magnet that drew her memory back. "We were beside ourselves with dread. I asked Pastor Ben to announce that we needed prayer for you. Everyone rallied around, asking God to fix whatever was wrong, and that you wouldn't die."

The look of remembered despair in Mom's eyes clutched at my heart. I'd always loved her as my mother; now I saw her as a fellow human, suffering under the weight of worry for her baby.

Mom avoided making eye contact as she recalled the gut-twisting memory. "The doctor put you in the hospital for three days for tests. The hardest part of the whole ordeal was leaving you each night, sobbing and holding out your arms to us as we left the room."

"Even though we waited just a few days for the test results, it seemed like a year. I don't think we could have made it through that dreadful time if not for all the prayers of our church family. Finally, the doctor called and told us he'd been wrong. You didn't have leukemia; only acute anemia. After they gave you iron supplement shots, you finally got some color—for the first time in your life—and they sent you home."

"So, the doctor made a huge mistake in his original diagnosis?" I asked, my cheeks heating with anger. "That seems pretty irresponsible of him."

Mom walked to her dresser and slid the photo into the corner of the mirror's frame. "Well, doctors are human, too. I wasn't mad at him—he did the best he could with the knowledge he had. I was just glad to have my baby girl back. And although he felt he'd made a mistake in his diagnosis, I've always been convinced that the Lord healed you in answer to our prayers."

Finally, Mom allowed herself to look at me, her smile a gleaming jewel. "When we brought you home, you kept running around patting everything—your crib, your rocking horse, your daddy's chair. You couldn't say so, but I knew you were as relieved and excited as your Daddy and I that you were finally home."

I got up and walked to the mirror, taking one last look at the picture before saying hopefully, "You never did tell me the award I got for the baby pageant, Mom. Was it the Most Beautiful Baby?"

Her eyes shone with a queenly beauty. "No, honey, it was the Healthiest Baby award."

My childish dream of a movie-star body vanished that day with the wave of a tiny scepter. But a nobler, more mature dream replaced it. Thanks to Mom's example of faith and prayer, my healthy body would testify of God's mercy, turning a sick baby into a healthy princess.

3. A Jolly Miracle

As I dialed my friend Sandra, I tried to calm down. But it was no use. The minute she answered, I started bawling. "It looks like you'll have only three cats to take care of while we're gone next week. I think we're going to have to put Jolly to sleep."

"Oh, Jeanette, no! What happened?"

As I paced with the phone, sobs burst from my throat, my voice ragged. "Well, he was acting lethargic last night, he wouldn't eat, and his eyes were dull. I thought I should get him to the vet before we left on our trip so you didn't have a sick cat on your hands for nine days. The vet says he has a urinary tract infection and a liver problem that requires ten days of antibiotics. Jolly won't let anyone near him to give him the meds, so they refused to keep him there."

I stopped long enough to wipe the tears from my face. "I can't cancel this speaking trip; I committed to the writers conference five months ago. We leave tomorrow—that's too late for the conference director to replace me. And I can't ask you to give food and medicine to this cat for nine days in addition to feeding all three of my other cats and cleaning out their boxes too. That would be presuming on our friendship."

Sandra's voice was calm and low. "No, no, no, that isn't presuming at all. I can give Jolly the meds; I've done it with my own cat. How old is he, anyway?"

"Only two. He's my baby. After Angus—my favorite cat ever—disappeared three years ago, I made a vow to myself that I'd never love another cat like I loved him. But I couldn't help myself with this little guy. He stole my heart." I told Sandra how Jolly let me carry him around, nuzzling his head next to my cheek. He even seemed to relish the silly kitty/baby talk I used just for him. I would often hold him up in the mirror and say, "Are you mama's baby?"

Before he got sick, I would've been embarrassed to admit to anyone that I acted that way over a cat, but now it seemed not so silly after all.

"Well, we're not gonna give up on him that easy, Jeanette. I'll come over tonight and you can show me what to do, okay?"

I released a thankful sigh, but my heart still felt like cement. "Okay—see you tonight. And thanks again—you're a jewel."

When I came through the door from work, my first words to my husband were, "Where's Jolly?"

"I'm not sure. We had a horrible time transferring him from the cage at the vet's into the carrier—he growled, clawed, even hissed at me. The vet's assistant was afraid of him."

I argued as I hunted for my fur baby. "He was scared, Kevin. If a stranger shaved your arm and stuck needles in you, then put you in a cage overnight, you'd be none too thrilled with them either. Oh, here he is."

Jolly lay curled in a fetal position on the floor of my closet, his eyes turned down at the corners. He was too weak to cry, but when he saw me kneel down beside him, he started purring.

"Oh, Jolly," I said, "I'm so sorry you're sick. Please don't die, okay? I love you so much. Please get well." While I stroked his head and back, I alternated between begging Jolly to recover and asking God to heal him. When Sandra rang the doorbell twenty minutes later, I was lying on the carpet next to Jolly, all thoughts of dinner and my upcoming trip erased from my mind.

While Sandra was asking about our trip, I managed to squirt a syringe-full of mustard-colored medicine into the side of Jolly's mouth. The whole time he swallowed it, he growled at me. "I'm sorry, honey," I crooned, "but this nasty-tasting stuff will make you better." He soon drifted off to sleep. I woke up a dozen times in the night, hoping I'd find him still alive in the morning.

When I peeked into the closet at daybreak the next morning, I found an empty spot where he'd been. I tried to give him another dose of medicine before we left town. He growled at me and spit it out. "I hope we're doing the right thing by leaving him," I moaned to Kevin. "What if he won't let Sandra give him any medicine?"

Kev paused and took my hand. "I think he'll be okay, Jeanette. Sandra will take care of him. And so will God."

I sighed and squeezed my eyes shut to keep the tears from dripping out.

We'd barely left the driveway when I texted Sandra. "No meds down Jolly. Hope you can manage it 2nite. Thx again!"

Over the next nine days, I tried not to fret while traveling the gorgeous Ohio and Pennsylvania highways, visiting with our son, and speaking to aspiring writers. Sandra's texts to me didn't help much. "Jolly purrs when I feed him, but growls when med dropper appears. Sorry!"

Forcing myself to push aside mental images of returning home to a kitty funeral, I repeatedly prayed the only thoughts I could muster, "Please heal my baby, Lord."

As we pulled into the driveway, I asked Kevin to let me out before he drove into the garage. "I can't wait to see Jolly," I cried.

When he heard my voice, Jolly came running from the den to greet me, purring loudly and rubbing up against my ankles. I scooped him into my arms and sunk my face into his neck. "How have you been, buddy? Did you miss me?" I glanced at the bottle antibiotics sitting on the kitchen counter—almost full, just like it had been nine days before.

"Let's try this," I said, squirting some medicine into a spoonful of wet food. He lapped it up like he hadn't eaten in days. "Honey, come see this!" I hollered to Kevin.

Kev stopped unpacking the car long enough to raise his eyebrows in a question.

"Jolly is eating this medicine in food. Why didn't I think of this before? Sandra's been trying to get it down him this whole time by squirting the syringe in his mouth."

"But Jeanette," Kevin said, "I wonder if he needs the medicine now, however you get it down him. He looks as healthy as ever."

I took a hard look at Jolly then, standing on his hind legs, scratching at the back door to go out, catch a mouse, and bring it to me as a welcome-home gift. When I opened the door, he bounded onto the lawn.

"You're right, honey—he is back to normal. But I'll give him the meds till they're done anyway, since I paid so much for them."

I felt silly that it never occurred to me to put the medicine in Jolly's food to begin with. But perhaps it's a good thing—I mean a God thing. It gave the Lord an opportunity to show me how much He cares.

As I watched my little fur baby skitter across the lawn like a shooting star going sideways, I wiped the happy tears away, thankful for our Jolly miracle.

3. Back in the Ministry

After fifteen years of ministry, I had grown weary. I daydreamed of sitting in the pew each Sunday as a "normal" person. No Sunday school teaching, no song leading, no living our lives under the bifocals and magnifying glasses of every church member. Then, poof! My wish was granted.

When Kevin could not find a pulpit after leaving a successful youth ministry, he was hired at a small business office in downtown Los Angeles. Finally! I was free to be "myself." I could speak my mind on any subject without fear of disapproval. At last, I wouldn't have to set a sterling example or be stuck on anyone's rickety pedestal.

But soon, the truth slapped me in the face. I realized that whether I am wearing a hat labeled "pastor's wife," "homeschool mom," or "office manager," people will judge me, criticize my family, and have unrealistic expectations of me, *simply because it is human nature to do so.* I could not run away from scrutiny and hurts by leaving leadership behind. I just exchanged one set of challenges for another—which included the fact that Kevin was miserable.

Oh, he did an excellent job at the office. In fact, in ten years, he worked his way from bottom-rung office assistant to senior administrator. His boss regularly complimented him, saying what a pleasure it was to work with "a perfect gentleman." He brought Kevin gifts from his many overseas trips and raised his salary every year.

Nevertheless, Kevin's heart was not in answering phones and balancing accounts. He yearned instead to answer some deep, eternal questions and help people balance their lives by the power of the God's Word.

Repeatedly he confessed to me his need to be more content, to be thankful for his job and simply enjoy his relationship with the Lord. I admired his mature attitude. But, as I observed his growing longing to be back in the pulpit, I knew what I had to do.

So I gulped real hard, dashed away my tears, and said, "Lord, if my attitude is holding Kevin back, if my unwillingness to be a minister's wife is keeping him from getting another church, then I surrender. I cannot stand to see him unhappy like this. He's doing a fine job in the business world, but You didn't create him for this. He was made to communicate Your Word and Your love to Your sheep. If You want him to preach again, I'll not stand in Your way. Your will be done, not mine."

No angel choirs appeared, singing and dancing around the ceiling. No pearly rose blossoms sprinkled from the sky. And I did not hear God's voice say, "Good girl. I am well pleased with you." I just knew He was, and that was enough for my heart to rest.

Several months later we were back in the ministry.

I'd like to tell you that because I surrendered to God's will, He honored my obedience by making our lives trouble-free, persecution-free, and stress-free. I would also love to tell you that since we returned to the ministry, I have never doubted my call or wavered in my commitment to my husband or the Lord. If I did, however, I would be lying.

What I *can* say is that God has shown Himself faithful in every trouble, persecution, and stress. I hope that fact encourages you. Because if God can turn me into a preacher's wife and use me to change lives, He can move any mountain in your life. Are you ready?

4. True Confessions of a Hypocrite

"I am such a hypocrite!" I moaned to Kevin.

"What do you mean?"

"Oh, I sit and teach Sunday school every week, giving victory lessons to the ladies in my class. Then, when a crisis hits, I worry and fret. Or, if I have a rough day at work, I complain about how stupid people are. It's easy for me to solve everyone else's problems, but solving my own is like asking the Rolling Stones to sing "Take Me Out to the Ball Game!" Last week I taught the Women of Faith Circle about controlling fleshly appetites. I even gave them a list of Scriptures about keeping the body under control so they could read and meditate on them. Then today at the potluck after church, I scarfed down ten million homemade persimmon cookies!"

"That many?"

I gave him a nasty look. "I'm serious, Mr. Funny Pants. Why can't I live for ten minutes in a row what I preach?"

"Well, Jeanette, I think you're being too harsh on yourself. It's always simple to look at another's problem and objectively share a solution. We all do it. At least you realize the areas God is convicting you of, however. You are aware of your hypocrisy, and that's a good thing. No one except Jesus can say, "Follow me; I do all things well.""

"Great, I'm really encouraged by that. It's like saying, 'If you know how stupid you are, that's halfway to being smarter.' I just want to be grown up. I don't want to go through the process of getting there."

"Hmmm..." Even Kevin didn't have an answer for that one!

All the faults of others that annoy me? They stare at me from the mirror every day. Why am I so irked by people who yak their faces off, never allowing anyone else to talk? Why do Winnie Whiner and Gladys Griper irritate me so? Why do Slothful Sally's dusty corners and unmade beds make me want to go home and find my can of Comet cleanser?

Whenever I gossip or complain about someone else's faults, the Holy Spirit pokes me, asking, "And you're so perfect?" I *never* get away with complaining.

One day I was complaining to the Lord that I never get away with complaining. "Lord, look at Doodly Doo who is an elder down at Three Spires Church on the corner. He is grumpy with his employees, treats his wife like a dog, and never mows his lawn. How come You let him get away with all that, and I can't get away with anything?"

God is so sweet. He remained as calm as a midnight sea when He answered, "My dear, do you really want to get away with things? Or, do you want Me to love you enough to tell you when you are hurting Me, yourself, and those you care about?" I think He even smiled when He said that. At least, the tone of His voice had a smile in it, like the dentist's when he sits down on the stool the size of a lily pad, and talks to you about the x-rays of your cavities. He and God are just doing their job. They know they are about to tell you something you really don't want to hear, so they try to make it as pleasant as possible.

I forever fail to win an argument with God! But I had to admit He was right. I really don't want to get away with attitudes and actions that hurt Him or others. So, I bring Him the same stinky sins over and over, relying on His forgiveness and cleansing.

Will I always be a hypocrite? Probably.

I can't imagine myself at the place where I can say, "Let me get that speck out of your eye, honey," without the bitter stab of conviction that I'm peering around a log. But if Kevin's word is any consolation, at least I'm showing a little maturity by not pretending to be perfect!

5. Surprise!

I have orchestrated two surprise birthday parties for Kevin, and he found out about both beforehand, so I gave up. But I know someone who loves surprises as much as I.

God does. He delights in surprising us. I think He enjoys doing things in unexpected, out-of-the-ordinary ways, because we need to be reminded that He is still in the miracle business, and we needn't worry if our problems seem more impossible than the next guy's. He can fix anything with one little surprise.

I'll bet Daniel was surprised when those lions that the king had him thrown in with went to sleep! And, don't you think the disciples were surprised to see Jesus walking on the water in a vicious squall? Or, when He raised a widow's son from his coffin in the middle of the funeral procession? And, the surprise to clinch them all was when God resurrected Jesus after He'd been dead three days. Now, that's something to party about!

God has given me a few notable surprises in my lifetime. When I was seventeen and thought I had sinned far too much for Him ever to forgive me, I came across a verse in Hebrews 10:17 (NASB) that told me, "Their sins and their lawless deeds I will remember no longer." God was saying, "Surprise! I love you in spite of your failings! I do want you in my family!"

When I was eighteen, my friend Brad told me that his friend, Kevin, needed a wife. I agreed to pray for Kevin, and a year after meeting him, God said, "Surprise!" when He used me to answer my own prayer.

Eighteen years ago when my son and I were getting on the freeway in LA to go to the grocery store, we prayed that God would let us live in the country someday. By the time we got the call to come to Paris, Illinois, I had forgotten that prayer. I wanted to stay in Southern California with my great friends, prestigious job, and 235 restaurants to choose from. But God had not forgotten. Surprise! We are happier here than we have ever been in our lives.

When I get into a mess, whether it's one of my own making or someone else's, I remind myself of God's ability and willingness to surprise me. I need to keep James 1:17 in the forefront of my mind: "Every good and perfect gift is from above, coming down from the Father of the heavenly lights."

He loves to jump out when we least expect Him, and turn impossible situations around. He loves to change stubborn hearts, heal incurable cases, rescue people from prison, restore what's broken, and fix the worst problems imaginable. The bigger the mess, the more fun He has surprising you when He steps in and unscrambles it. His resources are unlimited, and His ideas are the cleverest.

Next time you come up against a stubborn mountain that refuses to move out of your way, instead of saying with everyone else, "You can't win for losing," say "God, I'm ready for a surprise!"

6. Imagine That

"Do you have grandchildren? Tell me about them."

I needed a distraction. To prepare me for cesarean surgery, the kind, sixtyish nurse was fighting to find a vein large enough to put an IV in. She was on the fourth try, and my arm had had enough. I closed my eyes to pray while she talked about her darlings. "Please, Lord, open that vein," I begged, while imagining a picture in my mind of a vein tightly shut. I saw it spiraling open, growing large enough to let sunlight in. Suddenly the nurse exclaimed, "We got it! At last!" I sighed and thanked the Lord.

I had just discovered a method of prayer I've used many times since, that of imagining what you are asking God to do. It's a little "faith-helper." But it works in a big way.

Most of us leave the world of imagination when we leave childhood. Our adult world is full of the realities of earning a living, holding together relationships, and staying healthy. We rarely use our imagination apart from decorating a room, planning a garden, or dreaming of a vacation.

Yet God gave us the wonderful tool of imagining for us to use all our lives. It's not simply for artists, writers, or architects, but for everyone. He gave us our ability to see something before it actually takes place as a way of helping Him bring it about.

I'm sure this is what the chronically sick woman in Mark 5 did. She told herself, "If I just touch his clothes, I will be healed" (Mark 5:28). No doubt she saw it in her imagination a thousand times, followed through on that thought, and it became a reality for her. Power went out of Jesus through His robe, and it instantly healed her of a malady she'd had for twelve years.

Jesus told a man, "Let it be done just as you believed it would" (Matthew 8:13). The writer of Hebrews tells us, "Faith is confidence in what we hope for, and assurance about what we do not see" (Hebrews 11:1). That assurance must be in our hearts and minds for it to become real.

We can help our prayers along by visualizing the answers. This is not mere "positive thinking." This is using the brain God gave us to speed up the fulfillment of the dreams and plans He's put in our hearts. If we ask God for a happy marriage, a growing church, or wisdom on the job but don't expect Him to give it to us, what's the point of asking? But if we visualize it happening as we ask, and keep the picture before us as the woman in Mark 5 must have done, we create expectancy in our hearts that draws God's favor to us.

God wants your family to know Him and be in heaven with you. He wants your marriage strong, your finances in good shape, and your body healthy. In other words, He wants you to have an abundant life. He is a good God Who gives only good gifts. But He wants us to ask, in faith. And sometimes our faith needs a little help. So He's graciously given us just the help we need, right inside our minds.

Imagine that!

8. A God for All Seasons

"No, I can't wear that dress to church, Mommy. It's a Christmas dress, and today isn't Christmas!"

Our friend's six-year-old daughter, Sally, insisted that the lovely dress she'd already worn for Christmas could not be re-worn on December twenty-seventh, or any other day of the year. She pulled out the same stubborn attitude with the costly Easter dress her parents bought her a few months later. Both garments hung useless in the closet, worn only once. Sally missed the enjoyment of those beautiful clothes because she misunderstood the purpose of them. (If it were my daughter, I'd stop buying expensive dresses and switch to yard sale clothes, but I'll save that for another book).

After praying in the Garden of Gethsemane, Jesus "returned to his disciples and found them sleeping. 'Couldn't you men keep watch with me for one hour?' he asked Peter" (Matthew 26:40). Many people have made a rule of this question. They maintain that we must spend at least an hour a day in prayer, implying that we are lacking in faith if we pray any less than sixty minutes.

If we make praying a rule and set the timer like we would for a casserole, we limit our relationship with God. We neglect His companionship throughout the day, thinking, "I've given God my hour," or "I went to church on Sunday." This attitude is

But we prayed and threw ourselves on the mercy of the Lord. Within one year, the hospital and doctor bills were fully paid.

"How'd that happen?" asked Ron.

"I don't even know. Someone gave us a $100 gift, but apart from that, the Lord just provided little by little, till it was all paid off. I can't explain it. If I could, it wouldn't be a miracle."

"Another time, when Dad was youth pastor in Northern California, he was told the church had run out of money. They gave him one month's notice, and then his salary would stop. It normally takes a lot longer than one month to find a new ministry, sometimes a year or more. But God came through again. We were hired at the church in LA the same Sunday Dad preached his trial sermon, and they paid him for his first week in advance. We didn't even miss a paycheck!"

I paused while my brain retrieved memories of other miracles. "And do you remember the Peugeot?"

Ron rolled his eyes. "How could I forget that crappy car? It was in the shop for repairs more than it was out on the streets."

"Well, do you recall how one night when we sang at a church in Orange County, Dad mentioned we were having trouble with our car? The next day the pastor called us, asking us to come there and pick up a check some anonymous man had left for us."

"Oh, yeah. That was the check for $3,000, wasn't it?"

"Yes—from a total stranger! When I told the mechanic at the Peugeot repair shop about it, he nearly fainted from shock. It was a huge witness to him of how God takes care of His kids."

I continued for twenty minutes, rehearsing the many times God had come through when we were in trouble, with nowhere to turn for help but to Him. Most of our miracles involved finances, but others were sticky relationship issues that needed resolving, or physical healings. The picture was one of our loving Father's involvement in every area of our lives. Nothing was untouched by His hand of grace.

As I preached to my son, I gained confidence myself that God would provide for our current need.

A few days later, a lady from our homeschool group, who'd heard we were looking for a home, contacted me. The house they had for rent was perfect for our needs and only three miles from my new job. We moved in just days before escrow closed on our mobile.

The writer of Proverbs says, "Death and life are in the power of the tongue (18:21 NKJV)." When we rehearse God's miracles to others—and to ourselves—our words become a cheerleading squad to infuse hope and strength into our sagging souls, giving us courage to trust Him for our current challenge.

Do you need a home, a harvest, or a healing? Rehearse God's miracles, and then watch Him work!

10. Don't Do It Oh-Self

When my brother Daniel was a toddler, his desire for independence caused him to refuse help with everything from putting on his clothes to combing his hair. After he was told, "Oh, all right, do it yourself then," his favorite phrase became "Do it oh-self!" I imagine Mom was frustrated at times with his stubbornness. But it was also a healthy sign. As parents, we are happy when our children desire to be independent. No one wants to be tying the shoes of a fifteen-year-old or wiping a thirty-year-old's nose.

But I think our heavenly Father has the opposite attitude about us as His spiritual children. God delights in helping us. He never thinks, "What is wrong with you? Why can't you do life by yourself? I have babied you through forty-nine years with wisdom, protection and blessings, and I'm tired of it by now. When are you going to grow up?"

No. No. *No!* The most mature attitude we can have as Christians is one of utter dependence on God in every area of our lives. We came into God's family completely helpless. We became His by admitting we were powerless over the sin in our lives, acknowledging that only He could cleanse us. Then we humbled ourselves, asking Him to remake us and fill us with His goodness. What craziness makes us think that after He saved us, He expects us to travel through life by our own wits?

I have naturally curly hair, but that doesn't mean the curls go the direction I want. Seventy-nine percent of the time I find myself standing in front of the mirror at 8:15 in the morning with my pick in one hand and my super sculpt gel in the other, begging God to make my curls cooperate. If I didn't have this little talk with Him, you would not want to see the results!

It's the same with driving, especially when I'm behind someone who makes me wonder if they got their license in a box of Lucky Charms. If I leave God out of that equation, I may call someone a name no preacher's wife has any business using!

What about relationships? Is *anyone* easy to live with? I don't care how good they smell or what sweet things they say when you are dating them; after you unpack from the honeymoon, you find out the true meaning of "opposites attract." There is simply no way two people can live in the same house and get along halfway civilly without the help of Almighty God. You can't do relationships oh-self!

And most of all, I need help getting fixed when I am broken. We all have our own way of trying to put emotional Band-Aids on scars of the soul. It could be drinking too much, watching soap operas, getting into one bad relationship after another, or even using drugs. With me, it's overeating and showing off to get attention. Oh, I almost forgot—spending money to make myself feel loved and important. But I found out, as you may have, that none of those things cuts it. I simply don't have the right tools to fix myself. And neither do you.

But, hey, good news: God made us both. He knows the deep places in us that hurt, even places we are not aware of. He was there when we got broken, and He knows exactly what it will take to make us whole again. Whether we were hurt by someone's cruel words, unkind treatment, or neglect, or we hurt ourselves through rebellion and sin, God is the only One Who can fix us properly.

Paul tells us in Romans 8:32 that because God willingly gave up His own Son for us, He will also willingly give us everything else we need. If the need is self control not to swear at a stupid driver, wisdom for a tough relationship, or help in mending your broken heart, don't try to do it oh-self. God is waiting to help you.

Just be mature enough to ask.

11. How Prayer Journaling Keeps Me Sane

"Sandy told me I should keep a journal about this horrible time I'm walking through," I told my friend Rachel, "but it's just too painful to write about."

Rachel agreed with Sandy. "Even if you write just one sentence a day, it will help you get a grip on your feelings, and that'll be a start. You don't have to write a book; just a sentence."

When I finally took their advice, I was amazed at how much healing I experienced because of this simple yet powerful exercise. It's become a soothing friend in my anguish, a haven to run to when I'm overwhelmed. And since no else sees it, it's safe from anyone who might be offended by my candor.

What factors about journaling our prayers help us when we're in the midst of a super-sized problem?

It's cathartic

Getting our feelings and impressions down on paper allows us to analyze our situation objectively. As long as our emotions stay locked away in our souls, we can't find answers for what hurts us. When we allow ourselves to say, "I'm mad at Mom when she embarrasses me in public," or "My kid's choices scare me," we can begin to seek the healing we need.

It's empowering

When we share what's been stuck inside, even if it's ugly, we're allowing God to get involved in our lives on a deeper level. We're opening our hearts to His voice—thus to His wisdom and love. We might even choose to write down what we feel He's saying to us in answer to our cries. That's when we start to heal.

It's faith-building

Weeks, months, and years from now we have a record to look back on. We see how the Lord brought us out of calamity or gave us wisdom in a sticky situation. That builds our faith to expect Him to move again when another mountain stands in our way.

It's enlightening

Journaling helps us gain fresh ideas and insights. As we write, we prime the pump of creativity and ingenuity. We leave behind yesterday's thoughts and the stale, unoriginal ideas of the negative people who surround us. We open our minds to the bottomless well of God's mind and heart so He can show us how to think and behave like He does. Wow!

It's cheap

My friend and fellow writer Jim Watkins reminded me of this fun benefit: "Journaling is cheaper than a therapist. My journal always listens to me and never judges me, even if my ramblings could be used as possible evidence in a sanity hearing." So . . . if you can't afford a therapist, write your problems down, and let the healing begin.

12. Go for the Chunks

"This isn't the same as yesterday, Grandma. I want the chunky kind."

On the day in question, I had made the mistake of giving 4-year-old Jenessa some of my expensive frozen yogurt, the kind bursting with lovely slices of real peach. The plainer, peach *flavored* kind I offered her the following day wasn't cutting it. From now on, she'd be unwilling to settle for less than the best.

Just as Jenessa was not embarrassed to ask me for the chunky kind of yogurt, we also should not be embarrassed to ask God for blessings in our lives. It delights God to bless and help us. He longs to pour out His kindness and goodness on us. (See Isaiah 30:18.) So, we're actually doing Him a favor by asking Him to do us a favor!

I popped over to the church a few mornings ago to pray. I didn't have much time, so I told the Lord I wouldn't ask Him for anything; I'd just praise Him. "Go ahead," I could hear Him encourage, "I want you to ask." What a great Father!

Seeking God's blessings is not prideful or selfish; it is a command! In Matthew 7:7, Matthew 21:22, and Mark 11:24 we are told by Jesus Himself to ask God for whatever we want. *Not*, "Ask Me for something if you feel worthy." *Not*, "Ask Me to bless you if you've been particularly kind and loving today."

Not, "Ask Me for a favor if you've gone to church every Sunday this year and have been reading the Bible faithfully."

If your very wealthy boss came to you and said, "I like you. I have decided to give you a raise. Whatever you ask for, I will do it," most likely you'd not say, "Oh, no, there are other people here doing a better job than I. It would be selfish of me to take your money. I'll just stay at my current pay rate and be content."

If a millionaire relative died and left you everything, you would not refuse it, allowing the State to take it. No one would accuse you of being mean and greedy for receiving what is freely offered by a generous person, even if you didn't think you deserved it.

If we will accept blessings from one another, why refuse them from a loving, giving God? Especially when He's the One telling us to ask!

Some people think eternal life is the only benefit we should expect from being born again, that we should never ask God for material or physical blessings. This implies that if someone does have material blessings, they earned them singlehandedly, and God had nothing to do with it. If you have a fine car, extra money in the bank, and a house full of beautiful furniture and say, "But, by golly, I never asked the Lord for a penny of this!" how does God get the glory in that?

Yes, living in heaven in God's presence is the most precious blessing God could and did give us when we said yes to Jesus. But that same Jesus said, "I came that they may have and

45

enjoy life, and have it in abundance [to the full, till it overflows] (John 10:10 AMP)." The apostle Paul seconded Jesus' motion by saying, "God gives us richly all things to enjoy (1Timothy 6:17 NKJV)." And besides, the more God blesses me with, the more of a blessing I can be to others. I can't help fund your mission trip, buy you groceries, or put money in the offering at church if I'm barely getting by. In order to be a blessing, we must be blessed. And God requires that we ask.

Go ahead: make God's day. He is eager to pour out His favors on you. Be bold enough to go for the chunks!

13. A Modern Miracle

Do you believe in miracles? How do you define one?

A person like my Dad, for instance, a three-pack-a-day man, flushes all his cigarettes down the toilet after smoking for thirty-five years and never craves another smoke. Does that seem like a miracle? Or, a couple who cannot conceive for over ten years of marriage suddenly turns up pregnant. That causes me to praise the Lord. How about a recovery from cancer or another Devilish, life-threatening disease? Few would argue against the claim that those qualify as bona fide miracles.

I was the recipient of a freaky miracle several years ago that still amazes me. . .

If you get to know me for more than a week, you'll discover that I've always detested housework. I am all about creativity, variety, and fun. Mopping floors and dusting furniture could never compare with taking my grandkids to the zoo, planning a party, or trying a new restaurant. We don't live in filthy conditions; just not as clean as I imagine heaven is. But that's another chapter.

Early in our marriage, I tried a 3-x-5 card system to organize my daily, weekly, and monthly chores. I accomplished them all right, but they were still chores. I was bored out of my wits every time I picked up a mop or pushed a sweeper.

When my kids got old enough to help, I transferred the mop and the sweeper to them and paid them to drudgerize. Worked beautifully! They earned some money, I got a clean house, and they learned to be diligent and responsible. By the time they were teenagers, the only thing I did was the cooking, changing the sheets on Kevin's and my bed, and washing our laundry.

So I had a discourteous awakening when Marie went to college, and Ron was too busy with homework, guitar lessons, and high school friends to take on all of his sister's chores. *No problem,* I thought. I divided the tasks between Ron and me, and gave Ron a raise. A month later, I discovered something strange. Ron kept up on his extra chores, while my dust bunnies had great-grandbabies, and my kitchen floor got crumbier than a highchair tray on a baby's first birthday. Now what?

When Ron went off to college, I became a desperate pastor's wife. How could I manage a full-time job, be a supportive spouse, and still have an uncluttered house? As a last resort, I did something that shocked even me: I prayed that I would enjoy housework.

I can't put my finger on the day or the hour when I realized, "Hey, I'm having fun dusting and vacuuming and folding clothes; what's up?"

Then I remembered my prayer and realized I had a true-blue miracle on my hands: God had literally changed my heart! I was a cheerful cleaner at last!

Why do you suppose it took me thirty years to figure out that prayer was the answer to my dirty dilemma? Because I was proud of my aversion to spotlessness! I was determined with all my redheaded resolve that I was not going to give up my position on the board of the "I Hate Housework" club. Even though I was unhappy with myself and my surroundings, I still had to try to fix it in my own way. And it didn't work.

Friend, you don't have be that dense and stubborn! If you are in the midst of a problem you have tried to solve every way you can think of, don't wait until you are desperate and use prayer as a last resort. Cry out to God *today*! Ask Him to fix it, and then be open to your own heart being changed, if need be. If my thirty-year blunder can save you some heartache, it was well worth all the anguish and grime I went through!

There is nothing more miraculous than God changing a heart; let that happen to yours.

14. Little People

I had one of those days that you don't wish even on your grumpy landlord. My computer wasn't talking to my printer. After I spent two hours on the phone with tech support, they were friends again, but then the printer jammed. To accompany an article I'd written, I took photos of a church's vibrant stained-glass windows. The newspaper I freelanced for printed the photos in black and white. Black. And. White. For stained glass. Yep, one of those days.

And those days seemed to be happening more and more often.

Nearly a year before, our daughter had announced her divorce. The tumult that followed for her and her three young children tested my faith to its maximum stretching point. Then our son moved back home, and the depression he'd suffered for twenty-four years was freshly triggered by a bully at his new job.

I wasn't sleeping too well.

At my regular job as administrative assistant at a church, I usually sat in the assembly room to eat my lunch. One entire wall was filled with stained-glass windows—the central one of Jesus holding and blessing little children—in vivid color that no one can turn into black and white, even if they wanted to.

That window nourished my soul every time I gazed on it. Sometimes I saw myself as one of the kids in Jesus' lap, His hand on my head, blessing me. Sometimes I thanked Him for His bottomless mercy as I looked into the thoughtful set of His eyes. He wasn't smiling in this picture. He was empathizing with all the pains of growing up but still being a child. And I loved Him for that.

But on this very horrible day, after I'd eaten, I wandered down to the toddler's playroom in the church basement. I needed to be alone, to decompress from the rigors of adulthood with its computers and printers, from people who didn't understand that stained glass is art, and from adult kids' problems I couldn't fix.

Perhaps crying was somewhere on my agenda, too.

As I entered the door of this room bursting with color, I spied the best spot to sit—a quilt-covered rocking chair. I took a seat and let my eyes peruse the walls, where someone had taken great pains to letter "Jesus loves the little children" in several languages. Another kid-loving artist had stenciled pairs of animals leaving the ark—fun ones like butterflies, turtles, and capuchin monkeys. On the wall opposite me, baby handprints made to look like flowers winked and smiled.

I started to relax. Breathe. Soak in God's love.

Then to my left I spotted a set of bright yellow shelves with various toys, all sparkling clean. *Someone cares about these babies*, I thought to myself. Among the toys were bins of smaller playthings, all labeled in neat printing: "Blocks."

"Jungle Animals." "Little people." I smiled, remembering the happy hours my own children had spent decades ago with their "little people" toys. How simple life was in those days.

Then the Lord spoke.

I don't mean I heard an audible voice. But down in my heart, where I sometimes hide behind my pain and where I let only Jesus in, I could feel His blessed wisdom wash over my anger, frustration, and guilt. *We are all little people,* He seemed to say. *These problems and issues that seem so big to you— others have them, too. Your tangled troubles are not bigger than those of the other little people around you. Everyone counts. Everyone is important. But compared to My strength and love, everyone is little. Now, will you let Me hold you till the pain goes away?*

I lifted my heart to Him, allowing Him to shoulder the weight of my cares. I didn't have to fix everything. He was big enough to handle it all.

I may be mistaken. But when I walked up the stairs and through the assembly room to return to my office and I gazed up at Jesus and the children, I think He smiled at me.

15. Bart and the Breadsticks

Hot. Buttery. Comforting. Those breadsticks are the reason this Italian restaurant ranks as one of our favorites. Not only do they melt in your mouth and addict you after one bite, but the waiters also bring you fresh ones every five minutes. I never used to be a bread lover...

Tonight we were waiting for our main course when a young waiter came by with his familiar basket. We couldn't say yes fast enough. But when he asked how many we'd like and Kev said, "Four, please," he gave us the only two in the basket and said he'd be back!

"Why do you suppose he asked us how many we wanted, honey?"

"I don't know; just trying to be agreeable, I guess. Like your mom asking you if you wanted to clear the table when you were a kid, and when you said no, she told you, "Do it anyway. I was just being pleasant!""

Made no sense to me. But I was too far into breadstick heaven by that time to analyze it. I can make a breadstick last four or five bites, but Kevin gobbles his in two or three. (Why do you suppose men are like that?)

Then I thought about Jesus. And the blind man, Bartimaeus, who kept hollering after Jesus as He passed through the man's town: "Jesus, Son of David, have mercy on me!"

Jesus called for him and asked, "What do you want me to do for you?"

No hesitation: "Rabbi [Teacher], I want to see."

"Go," said Jesus, "your faith has healed you." And the man followed Jesus from then on. (See Mark 10:46–52.)

Jesus isn't at all like that waiter who offered us as much as we wanted, then told us we'd have to wait for more. "Oh, you need that much? I don't have enough in my basket right now. Just wait here; I'll be back!" When Jesus asks you what you want, He means it. No empty promises with Him.

Jesus' basket of favors is bottomless. He never runs out of anything you need. In fact, He has enough healing, money, wisdom, courage, and peace of mind for everyone who's ever lived.

But, can it be as simple as Bartimaeus made it? Just ask for what you need? Or, has Jesus changed?

Jesus has not changed. Not now, not ever. Hebrews 13:8 makes that very plain. He is still the Healer, the Bondage Breaker, the Savior and the Shepherd. So, if I'm not getting my prayers answered like I should, it can't be His fault.

Maybe my lack of faith is the problem; perhaps I don't really believe Jesus is willing to give me everything I could possibly need and want. Was Bartimaeus more convinced than I am of Jesus' gracious spirit? Perhaps I haven't been as persistent with my requests as Bart was. Even when people around him told him to shut up, he refused to quit crying out to Jesus until he got His attention. Or, maybe I haven't really made Jesus the Master of my life, jumping up to follow Him wherever He might lead me, like Bartimaeus did after Jesus set him free. I believe I need to do some soul searching.

After this last breadstick...

16. Hold for Faith

Don't you love those phone service menus that make you punch thirteen buttons to get to the person you want? "To place an order press 1, for accounting press 2, to yell at us for getting your order wrong, press 3..." Sometimes I wonder if there really are people at these companies' board meetings, or if there are just a bunch of numbers sitting around a table making decisions and policies.

I had a fun surprise a few days ago, however, when I called a company, and after punching in the proper numbers I heard, "Please hold for (pause) *Faith.*"

"Oh, neat," I thought, "They have the phone programmed to say the name of the person I'm going to talk to so I can address her personally. How cool is that!"

Then, while I was listening to the tunes they play for you that are intended to make you forget you are holding, I had another interesting thought: *We do have to hold for faith most of the time. It rarely comes in just a blink.*

The challenge usually isn't starting the race, or crossing the finish line. It's all those in-between times when you wonder if your faith will see you through to the end, when you question if you should have ventured out in the first place. You may even fear you won't finish at all, and everyone will know what pea-sized faith you really have.

Most of our lives are spent "holding for faith," aren't they? The victories are the goal of course, and God is rooting for us to have them. But it's the patient plodding during the waiting times that really impresses Him. If we refuse to give up on our dream or our prayer, no matter how long it seems to be taking, that makes Him proud that we are His children, because we are growing to be just like Him: strong and enduring to the finish. It's the waiting times where we prove to ourselves and the Devil what our true character is really like. I asked my husband, who has studied the Bible for forty years, why some prayers are answered so quickly and why some take years to come to fruition. His answer:

"I don't know."

Not exactly the answer I was looking for! But, I think it's great he's humble enough to admit he doesn't have all the answers. God does not always choose to tell us everything.

Often we don't know what God is doing and why He is making us "hold for faith" rather than giving us what we want right away. But if we will trust Him and refuse to give in to discouragement and the Devil's lies that God neither hears nor cares, more often than not we will find out why after we have crossed the finish line and our "faith becomes sight."

James tells us to "strengthen [our] hearts, for the coming of the Lord is near" (James 5:8, NASB). Although I may prefer not to "hold for faith," I love the results: my confidence in Jesus grows stronger by the minute.

17. The Great Zucchini Fiasco

"Why do I get myself into these fiascoes?" I mutter, as I wipe the kitchen counter for the fifth time, hoping the zucchini pulp's neon green doesn't stain.

The phone rings. It's my eleven-year-old granddaughter, who's the starter for our three-kids-and-two-grands Sunday chat. "Whatcha doin', Gramma?" she chirps.

"Oh, honey, I am up to my elbows in zucchini bread, zucchini muffins, and zucchini mini-loaves. I underestimated how much zucchini pulp would make a cup, so I had to triple the recipe."

She giggles before saying, "That sounds like a mess."

"You have no idea, dear girl. I started out with a large bowl, transferred the batter to a huge bowl, and then had to graduate the bright green goo to my enormous chili pot. I ran out of flour in my canister, so I substituted a chocolate cake mix for the final cup. I wish you were here to help me!"

We visit for a while as I cradle the phone on my shoulder and fill muffins cups and loaf pans. Finally, I sigh with pleasure. "How many loaves and muffins do you think I ended up with?" I ask, mentally daring her to guess right.

Her giggle zips across the airwaves again. "I don't know."

"Three large loaves, eight mini-loaves, and sixteen muffins. And there is still a fifth of a zuke sitting in the fridge wondering if I forgot it!"

I've often joked how I use gardening in the summer and baking in the winter as therapy, because those activities are cheaper than a therapist's fee. But the zucchini fiasco has me rethinking that philosophy. I spent three hours of my time mixing and baking, another hour cleaning up, and have yet to ask forty-seven people if they'd like to adopt a loaf or a set of quintuplet muffins to make their home complete. Isn't my time worth at least two sessions with a shrink—in an office devoid of green-stained counters?

The upside is, I have enough breakfast breads to last the winter, my grandgirl and I bonded a bit, and my neglected loaf pans felt needed.

But the next time I see a "Free Produce" table somewhere with an eighteen-inch-long zucchini, I will run the other way!

Did you ever feel like your life is one big fiasco? You may have misjudged the negative potential of a giant zucchini, a person, or a job. Now you feel like you're cleaning up myriad messes caused by your own naivety. And you're embarrassed or afraid to ask God to help you. If you're anything like me, you think, "I got myself into this—I'm the one who needs to get myself out of it."

That's not what God thinks.

Throughout the Bible—both the Old and New Testaments—we read accounts of fiascoes that God-fearing people got themselves into. Think Moses the murderer, King David the adulterer, and Peter the liar. Did the Lord say to them, "Well, you made your bed hard, now you have to lie in it"? No, no, and *no* again.

Instead, He stretched forth His hand of grace and love, lifted them from their self-imposed messes, and gave each a fresh start. And He'll do the same for you and me.

In Acts, chapter 10, we see that "God plays no favorites," which means He didn't rescue Moses, David, and Peter because He liked them best. They were His kids, they were in a muddle, so He helped them like any good father would. And He hasn't changed His MO or His heart of kindness.

Now, go ahead and ask. The Lord is far more willing to help you clean up your messes than you might have thought. He probably even has a secret formula for removing neon green stains from countertops.

18. Prayer Cues

"Things with my stepdaughter Jill have gotten worse," cried my friend Lisa at our monthly coffee date. "She's saying mean things to the other kids about her dad and tries to pick fights with him all the time. My youngest, Logan, heard her cussing the other day. I hate to say this, but it's a relief when she goes to visit her mom on the weekends." Lisa grabbed a tissue from her purse and wiped mascara from her cheeks. "I've treated her like my own child ever since I married Paul when she was only seven. Now she's morphed into a spiteful, angry teenager. I just don't know what to do."

I grasped Lisa's hands and closed my eyes to pray, but not before I noticed a fresh spate of tears splashing from her large brown eyes onto the keychain lying on the table. It held a photo of her blended family—her own children, her husband's kids from his first marriage, and the youngest son they shared. Seeing their picture bathed in Lisa's tears energized my prayer. When I finished, I promised to tack Jill's name above my kitchen sink, where I'd be reminded to pray for her often.

When I came through the kitchen door an hour later, I grabbed a bright sticky note and pen. Using Jill's name as an acrostic, I wrote "**J**oy in her heart from You, Lord; **I**nsight for Lisa and Paul; **L**ead other Christian teens to befriend her; **L**ove herself more.

The next time Lisa and I met, her eyes danced with excitement. "You won't believe how much more peaceful the atmosphere in our home is," she bubbled. "I can hardly believe it myself! Jill doesn't argue with Paul nearly as much as before, she helps the younger kids with their homework, and she even told me 'I love you' the other day. I know we have a ways to go, but at least I don't feel like I'm drowning in anguish now."

This time *my* eyes dripped with thankful tears. "Well, I'd love to take the credit for Jill's attitude change," I told Lisa, "but we both know it was the work of the Holy Spirit, in answer to our prayers. Even the idea of placing Jill's name above my sink and using it as a way to pray for specific items for her isn't original with me—it's something called 'prayer cues.'"

"Oh, really?" said Lisa, "Tell me more."

"Well, I heard about this method of remembering to pray for specific people and situations years ago. In a sermon on prayer, a preacher told how he used everyday activities as prompts. And you know me," I laughed, "I'm always on the lookout for the fun way to do anything. So I adopted the idea."

I told Lisa how, when I make the bed in the morning, I pray for protection over our family, using Psalm 91 as a basis. When I dress and put my makeup on, I recite health and provision Scriptures. And my bedtime routine is the cue to pray for our marriage. "I have no doubt that's one of the reasons we've been married so long," I continued, "You know some of the challenges we've faced."

We all need divine intervention—for God to perform miracles large and small—in our families, jobs, and personal lives. Yet we find ourselves thinking or saying, "I don't have time to pray!" If by prayer we envision long hours on our knees in the dinky hours of the morning, then we may be right. But we can train ourselves to utilize snippets of time to talk to the Lord as we go about the day, using prayer cues as a way to keep in contact with Jesus all day long.

I'm not saying we shouldn't spend hours at a time on our knees or take some extended time alone seeking the Lord for help and wisdom. But when we feel like we need more face-to-face time with God and can't seem to fit in those huge chunks, prayer cues may be a creative answer.

Unless the name of the person you're praying for contains sixteen letters!

19. Change *Me*, Lord

As Kevin and I walked to our car outside a music store, Kev began relating a detailed story about the singing group on the record he'd just purchased. Since he's a pastor, as well as a teacher at heart, Kevin's explanations are like verbal outlines. Point I, then sub-points A, B, and C, Point II, and so on. They aren't boring—just more detailed than my low-level patience will tolerate.

Finally I sighed louder than usual and blurted, "Honey, I am going to pray that God gives you a friend you can explain everything to your heart's delight. After twenty-five years of listening to all this detail on every subject, I'm exhausted!"

Kevin laughed and said, "Why don't you pray that God will give you the patience to listen to me?"

"Because I *don't want* to listen! I want God to give you someone besides me to talk to!"

He laughed again.

In the fifty-plus years I've known the Lord, I've tried this method hundreds—maybe thousands—of times. I tell God how I think He ought to answer a prayer. If someone should ask me, "Do you think you're smarter than *God*?" I'd reply, "Of course not!" Still, I forge ahead with my clever ideas of what plan would be best to solve an issue or fix a problem. I am so creative, I sometimes even give the Lord several options.

He rarely takes my advice. He always has a different plan up His sleeve. And it's always better than anything I can concoct. In the case above, He led Kevin to a men's Bible study where he can pontificate to his heart's delight, and they love listening to his wisdom. But God also convicted me that I did, indeed, need to change.

Recently I found myself saying, "Lord, please change me so I'm a more patient listener." And, surprisingly, I meant it! I'm sure the Lord will give me many interesting opportunities to exercise my new patience muscles, but that's okay. I trust Him. And I realize I need to change more than I need God to fit Himself—or Kevin's personality—into my plans.

Because His plans always work.

20. Pray Like a Cat

As I write this, five cats fill the hallways of our home. Actually, we only have one hallway, but it sounds classier to say they fill our hallways than "they lounge on our couches, climb on our drapes, and spread fur on our dark green rug in the dining room."

I'm not what some call a "Crazy Cat Lady." I've just always felt that one good cat deserves another. And I think cats provide the perfect stress relief. Nothing calms my troubled heart or soothes my nerves like stroking a purring cat.

The only time I shout *no!* loud enough to scare one into decent behavior is when they use a door jamb or the backs of my legs as a scratching post. Apart from that, I spoil them rotten. Even so, one of them manages to get better treatment than the others at mealtimes—mine, not theirs.

My oldest cat, Rocky, a longhaired orange-and-white beauty, sits at my feet while I eat, patiently waiting for any scrap of meat or milk product to fall from my hand. He doesn't whine, beg, or try to jump into my lap. He simply hangs out where he knows the goodies are, expecting his tenderhearted cat mama to come through once again. And I always do. At twenty-one pounds, he's the fattest cat in the neighborhood, thanks to his persistent, calm expectation of goodies at meal times.

When I have something to eat that's not suitable—like soup or spaghetti—Rocky never pouts or whines. He simply walks away, accepting of my "not this time, Buddy." He knows there'll be another meal in a few hours or the next morning.

Rocky's constant asking for food is a message to me that he knows I'll take care of him. It's a compliment of the highest kind. If he ever stopped asking and expecting me to share, I'd know there was something wrong with our relationship.

That huge cat is my example of the perfect pray-er. I know my heavenly Father has everything I will ever need to prosper me spiritually and in every other way—to make me fat in my inner being from the banquet he spreads before me every day—His Word and His spirit of grace. When I come to Him regularly and wait in His presence, He shares His food—His wisdom—with me. I don't need to whine or cry to get His attention. He loves and cares for me far more than I ever dreamed of loving Rocky. He is my Father. He's committed to my well-being.

Sometimes the things I ask for aren't good for me. Then the Lord kindly says, "Not this time, sweetheart." I am slowly learning to accept His no, knowing there'll be lots of yeses in my future. I refuse to worry that I might starve if, this one time, I have to go without. The longer I walk with His hand in mine, the more I trust His heart for me.

So, if you want to learn how to pray like a pro, find a cat like Rocky and take him home.

Section II
Prayers for You

How I love you, my friend.

I appreciate your giggles and smiles at my craziness, when others roll their eyes or shuffle their feet. You are willing to risk people thinking you're weird for finding my jokes funny. You get my nutty sense of humor. And you make me laugh, too.

I bless you for believing in me when I couldn't find the courage to believe in myself. During nights of self-doubt and despair, when all my visions lay limp and crushed at my feet, you held out your faith to me and never wavered in your confidence that God would use me and redeem all my messes. You brought light to my hopeless future and breathed upon my gifts, resurrecting them.

I thank the Lord for arranging our paths to cross and for using you to notice the stars in my heart, shining your own light of grace upon them, causing them to shine brighter.

You are making a positive difference in one life—mine— and I imagine many others. I say, "Thank you, thank you, thank God," for you. I bless you, my friend.

These prayers are for you. *

*These prayers were originally written for my female friends, but I encourage all males reading this book to feel free to change the pronouns to suit their own gender.

Prayer #1: When You Want to Give Up on Your Dream

Lord, You see my sister and Your child, weeping in grief over the dream that's grown in her heart for years and is now in danger of dying. Please have pity on her and heal her broken heart. Wipe her tears, put them in Your bottle of love, and lift up her eyes to see that You have a shining plan for her—that You can make a way in the wilderness.

Father, this friend and sister has nourished my soul and helped me stand when I've been ready to slump over in defeat. Please take some of the seed that she's planted in my life, and cause it to bear a harvest of hope in her heart.

Wrap Your arms around her, let her feel Your love and strength today, and give her new ears to hear what You are saying to her. Still the voice of the enemy that would like nothing more than to see her give up on what You have placed in her heart—the good plans meant to lead to Your fingerprints touching many lives through her.

Renew her vision, dear Father. Send people to encourage her and help her overcome the Devil and his minions of deception. Give her joy in spite of the pain, and send riches her way to meet her material needs. And Jesus, dear Savior and Redeemer of all mankind, redeem this trial to bring beauty from the ashes and fruit from the pain.

In Your precious name, so be it.

References to Scripture: Psalm 56:8; Galatians 6:7; Philippians 4:19; Isaiah 61:3

Prayer #2: When You Feel Trapped in an Unfulfilling Marriage

I remember a ladies' magazine years ago with a popular column called, "Can This Marriage Be Saved?" Lord, I feel tempted to ask if You can save my friend's marriage—a marriage that started out with hopes as bright as the stars, but whose light has dimmed and nearly died out.

It's not that she doesn't love her husband, Lord. But by neglect, insensitivity, and selfishness, he has snuffed out every gleam of hope she once swung upon. She's forgotten how to look up, Lord. Now she's barely trudging through each day, facing problems alone, raising their children by herself.

I know she wants her marriage to be preserved, dear God, but her husband isn't willing to work at change. Can You do something with a heart that isn't willing? Can You—will You—turn it in Your hand as channels of water, to do Your will?

I think of Abigail, married to a fool. I think of Sarah, whose husband gave her away to two kings so he'd stay safe. And Mary, who followed Joseph to Egypt with the newborn Jesus, trusting Joseph had heard from You. You honored all these women in spite of their spouses' decisions that affected them in traumatic ways.

Please do the same for my friend.

Almighty Source of staying power and support, cause my friend and her husband to agree with one another as You and Jesus agree so their hearts and minds will resound as one to praise You.

Increase her ability to hope in You again. Meet her deepest emotional needs in ways only You can. Teach her marvelous, custom-made ways to look to You as her source of joy and fulfillment.

Rescue this couple from earthbound complacency and plant their feet and hearts once again in the stars so they can dream and dance with You in heavenly places. Let their lives be a beautiful trophy of Your love poured out into two lives, making them one.

In Jesus' name, so be it.

References to Scripture: Proverbs 21:1; Romans 15:5–6; Colossians 3:1–2

Prayer #3: When a Loved One
Is in Prison or Jail

Lord, You see every silent tear not loosed from a heart drowning in pain, and You capture every tear set free from a mother's hurting soul. Give my friend release today, healing, soothing God. Set her wounded spirit free to trust You, even as her son lives behind bars of steel.

No metal forged by men's hands can keep Your power and love away. Send a divine measure of each to her son today. Assure him that You are with him, and don't intend to leave.

Give him a patch of beauty to gaze upon in a gray world, a way to see that You care, a note of music in the silent anger. Strengthen his heart against blaming others for his wrongs or condemning himself for his errors. Soften his heart to hear Your voice of kindness. Help him believe that You offer a million new chances to go his way and sin no more.

Protect him from the Evil One and his minions who whisper lies in the dark and the day. Keep him from wicked schemes and plots meant to harm him. Fill his mind with wisdom to choose rightly, everything from companions to games to reading material. Even though his past and present are grim, offer him hope that his future can be brighter than he ever thought possible.

Give my friend surprises of grace along her path strewn with thorns. Lift her feet from the way of sorrow. Pillow her thoughts on You. In spite of the tears, may her heart sing with joy in Your embrace. Rescue her from every "what if," proving that shame is not of You.

Send Your Spirit to renew the limp dreams and wounded aspirations of my friend and her son. Breathe Your wind on fires of hope to burn away despair. Release them both into the light of Your presence—a presence filled with hallelujahs for sins forgiven and joys restored.

In Jesus' name, so be it.

References to Scripture: Psalm 56:8; Hebrews 13:5; Ephesians 3:16; John 17:15; Jeremiah 29:11

Prayer #4: When You Need
Victory over a Habit

Father, the enemy has lied to my friend and convinced her that she can't help herself from remaining captive to a besetting habit. You say differently. You declare that she is complete in You. You say the Anointed One, Jesus, is in her—the One sent by You to help, heal, and restore her to the original state You intended, a state of freedom to obey and enjoy walking with You every day.

Your Word is the truth that will set her free. Lead her to the verses that will speak the most succinctly to her mind and empower her to overcome her flesh. May she boldly declare Your Word over her life, and as she hears it, may faith rise up in her heart.

Give her a will to humble herself before You and to put her body under, making it her slave, not mastered by its urges. Strengthen her by Your Word and Your Spirit to say *no* to cravings. Not a weak "we'll see," but a loud, resounding *no!* that forces the Devil to flee in terror.

I confront Satan on her behalf and tell him he has no place in my sister's body, mind, and soul. Jesus, Lamb of God, You purchased her from Satan's kingdom by Your own blood. She has a right to stay free of compulsions and habits. I enforce that right, in Jesus' name, and declare Your lordship over every area of her life.

Wash over her like waves, dear God, cleansing her of every desire not born of You. Replace ungodly urges with cravings to know You, to love You, and to stay in Your presence. Show her that she's complete in You, needing nothing outside of You to fulfill her.

As You cleanse her heart of wrong desires, clothe her with favor and crown her with Your glory and power. Use her as a light to help others find their way out of besetting sins. May she lead them into the joy of Your presence and the warmth of Your smile.

In Jesus' name, so be it.

References to Scripture: John 8:44; Colossians 1:27; John 10:10; John 8:31–32; James 4:10; 1 Corinthians 9:27; 1 Peter 2:9–10; Colossians 2:10; Hebrews 12:12

Prayer #5: When You Are Worried

Lord, my friend is not only worried; she's also mad at herself for worrying. She knows You've promised never to leave her or forsake her. Yet she frets and agonizes over everything, from what she imagines people think of her to the threat of cancer.

Her worries torment her, slithering at her feet and perching on her shoulders, hissing dark thoughts and cackling what-ifs. Very real what-ifs, Lord, or she would dismiss them as foolish.

Yet they are not more real than Your love for her, Your care for her. For You are her Good Shepherd.

Please reassure her that, should she entangle herself in the thorn bush of troubles or sickness, You will remove every thorn, pull her free, and carry her on Your shoulders to safety.

Convince her that if someone else should trick her into wandering from the path You've planned for her, if she should get lost and be unable to hear You call, You would search for her until You found her and brought her home.

Should a star fall from the sky and burn her, You would heal her. Should she jump to catch a star and fall down, You would bandage her bruises, pick her up, and help her stand.

Let her know that she is never far from Your help. Every beat of Your heart is for her; Your every breath is to see her prosper and be protected. You never abandon Your sheep. Never. Even when it seems You have walked away, You are still right there beside her, cherishing her, holding her close to Your heart.

Encourage my friend to doubt her worries and to believe Your love instead. Let her hear Your sweetest song that sings to her troubled soul, "I love you always, even to the end. I will never stop loving you. You are Mine, and I am yours. All will be well."

In Jesus' name, so be it.

References to Scripture: Hebrews 13:5; 1 Peter 5:7, John 10; Luke 15:3–7;
1 John 4:18

Prayer #6: When Your Baby Is Sick

Father, here is my friend with a sick baby. You know how the doctors have done all they can to repair what's wrong. But they have limits that keep them from knowing what to fix and how to fix it.

Not You, dear Lord. You are unlimited in Your wisdom, ability, and willingness to help. Because You created this child, You know exactly what it's going to take to heal her. So, I'm asking You, Sir, to stretch forth Your hand of might and glory and love and do what no doctor can do: make this baby's body and brain work right. Restore every organ, every cell, every atom to completeness.

In Jesus, I see Your mercy for children. When His helpers thought He'd be bothered by mamas bringing their little ones to Him, He corrected that narrow thinking. Then He put His wonder-working hand upon those sweet little heads and blessed them. He was You personified, which shows me that You long to bless these tiny ones when others push them away or don't have time for them.

I believe You will put Your hand on this wee one, as Jesus did the babies brought to Him. Make her right. Bless her as only You can do. I'm bringing her to You, Lord. I know You won't push me away.

And for my friend, dear Father, please overcome her fear, confusion, and anger. Wrap Your arms around her heart, enabling her to trust Your love. We know You are not the author of sickness, but You're the Healer. Heal not only her baby, but also heal her wounded, sagging soul. Fill her with hope for all her tomorrows.

In Jesus' name, so be it.

References to Scripture: Romans 8:1–2; Galatians 3:43; Philippians 2:9; Revelation 5:9; John 8:32; Lamentations 3:23; Ephesians 2:6

Prayer #7: When You're Condemning Yourself

Father, my sister needs a revelation of Your grace today. She's condemning herself for choices she's made or failed to make. She feels responsible for the pain in her own life, as well as in the lives of those she loves. She wonders at times if the trials she's going through are a punishment for some past sin or foolish action. The enemy of her soul has her convinced that if only she'd been wiser and more obedient, none of these awful circumstances would be happening.

Lord, deliver her from this torment. Shine the light of Your deep, constant love into her soul today. Convince her that the well of Your goodness is deeper than any sin or foolishness on her part. Enable her to believe that You can and will redeem whatever choices she's made, turning the plot of Satan meant to destroy her into an opportunity for Your favor to blossom.

No matter the legion of lies she has believed about herself, Your name and Your blood are more powerful. I speak Your name into her mind and heart for deliverance and freedom, dear Jesus. Pour the oil of Your Spirit into her mind and emotions to deliver her, please.

Guide her into the truth. Your Word is truth. Lead her to the portions of Your Word that will cancel the insecurities and doubts she's feeling. Send mature believers into her life—those who know You and understand Your limitless grace—to change her thinking. Reveal Yourself to her as You really are: full of compassion, with new mercies every morning.

Give her a picture of herself as royalty in You, seated next to You in heavenly places, taking authority over darkness and walking in Your light and freedom.

In Jesus' name, so be it.

References to Scripture: Psalm 139:13—16; Matthew 19:14; Colossians 1:15; Romans 15:13

Prayer #8: When Your Parent Faces the Sunset

Dear Father, please speak Your peace to my friend's heart and mind today. Calm the mega-storm that threatens to steal every drop of joy from her heart. Walk across the waves of fear, and overcome her despair with Your sweet voice of comfort and serenity.

At times like these, Lord, we are torn between asking You for a miracle of healing and releasing our loved one into Your embrace. We know that the death of Your godly ones is precious in Your sight, but we also know that You are a wonder-working God Who still heals. So, we aren't sure how to pray.

Will You please take the desires of my friend's heart into account—as well as those of the other family members concerned—as You decide what is best for everyone, loving Father? We weep to think of the empty place in our hearts without this loved one; we are even a bit envious of them being in Your presence while we have to stay in the mess here on earth. But most of all, we want them not to suffer.

If her dad's race is run, Lord, and he's accomplished Your plan for him, please let him go without pain from his mortal body into his immortal one, forever free from the ravages of disease. But if You still have work for him to do before he meets You face to face, then stretch forth Your hand to heal him, please, so he can finish the work You gave him.

Whichever You choose, Lord, may Your name be lifted up and glorified, and may my friend and her family be strengthened in Your love today. May they know You better at the end of this day than they did at the start.

In Jesus' name, so be it.

References to Scripture: Mark 4:39; Psalm 116:15; Hebrews 13:8; 1 Corinthians 5:3; Acts 4:30

Prayer #9: When You Are Offended

Dear Father, I grieve for my friend who wears her feelings like a sugarcoating. She strives to make everyone around her happy, yet she hides a heart that rips too easily when people are unkind or insensitive.

She internalizes others' attitudes and tone of voice. She imagines they dislike her and mean to hurt her. She allows their moods to become hers. She loses herself in their darkness. Oh, Lord, this is not the worthy plan You meant for her.

Give her confidence that if someone treats her poorly, it's because they don't know how precious she is. They don't see what You see—the completed handiwork of Your making, the beauty of Your imprint on her heart and life.

Lord, set her free inch by glorious inch. Heal the ragged tears in the fabric of her heart. Sew it together with threads of love and acceptance. Correct her thinking so she sees herself complete in You. Like no one else. Happy to be her.

Jesus, please show her that she can choose the condition of her heart and not be a slave to her feelings. You are her God. You say she's very good. You made her in Your image, not the mirror of others' junk, but the mirror of Your nature.

Lift her out of herself and into Your presence, where You affirm and care for her. Reveal to her through Your Word and Your Spirit how dear she is to You and Your kingdom.

You value her. You are more than enough to set her free from caring too much what others think or say. Your grace weaves its colors throughout her soul, robing her in Your righteousness, clothing her with Your heart of mercy.

In Jesus' name, so be it.

References to Scripture: Jeremiah 29:11; Psalm 139:13– 16; Jeremiah 31:3; Colossians 2:10; Genesis 1:26, 31; 1 Corinthians 12:18; Luke 15:22

Prayer #10: When You're Raising a Teenager

Gracious Lord, in these uncharted waters of raising a teenager, will You please keep my friend's ship from sinking or from crashing on the rocks of confusion, fear, and anguish?

Show her how to respond to her almost-adult daughter in every circumstance. Give her such insight that she is amazed at the words from her lips—words of reasonable boundaries, unconditional love, and supernatural wisdom. Cause her to feel Your presence guiding her every choice so she knows she's not alone.

Help her to remain strong when her child disagrees with her decisions and tries to persuade or even force her to change her mind. Give her a sense of authority from Your Word and Your Spirit to stand by her declarations and not waver.

For her son, I ask that You protect him from the fierce storms of peer pressure and lies that threaten to cause his faith to sink. Shine Your beacon of truth into his soul to guide him into waters of protection and peace. Send him godly, discerning friends and mentors who will influence him for Your kingdom, never toward the enemy's false promises of always smooth sailing. Especially give him godly men, full of integrity, as role models to show him the kind of loving, nurturing, Father and Captain You are.

Please fill my friend's mind with images of her son at Your throne, worshipping and serving You all his days. Erase the images of failure, defeat, and disobedience.

Make him a man of valor, a man of the Word, and a man of God—just like Jesus. Yes, Lord, work the life and nature of Your Son in this young man. Fulfill Your good plan for him. In Jesus' name, so be it.

References to Scripture: Luke 8:24; Philippians 1:9-11; Isaiah 58: 11-12; Ephesians 6:10-12; Psalm 91; Proverbs 27:17; Ephesians 4:15; Jeremiah 29:11

Prayer #11: When Your Pet Dies

Father of life, take my sister in Your arms today and speak words of comfort to her soul in the loss of her precious pet. You created this furry friend to bless and fill her life with joy. [Pet's name] has fulfilled Your plan well, giving my friend much laughter and companionship to brighten her days. Now he is gone, and the wound in my friend's heart is huge and painful.

Dear Jesus, please fill that gaping wound with Your love, as only You can. Remind my friend of the days and years of sweet fellowship she shared with her little pal. Bring memories that make her laugh and shake her head in wonder at the creativity of Your hand and the kindness of Your heart.

I know You are not mocking my friend's grief. In fact, You are weeping with her, for You alone share the depth of her sorrow. You, above all, know the wrenching pain of loss and separation, for on the cross You willingly chose to separate Yourself from the Father that we might have life through Your death.

Yet You told us You'd give us laughter for our tears and dancing for our mourning, the oil of gladness to replace our sorrow. I'm asking for that gift for my sister today, please. Turn her tears into smiles once again. Cause her memories of [pet's name] to fill her soul with delight. With each day that passes, ease the ache in her heart and renew her hope in You, gracious Lord.

And if You think it would help her healing, will You please send another pet her way? I know that no one can fill the place of [pet's name], but I'm sure there's a sweet someone out there who needs a loving mommy like my friend. You know the one, Lord. Bring him or her my friend's way, please, on just the right day in her life.

Then we'll look up to You and say, "Thanks, loving Lord," for we know You are the giver of all good gifts.

In Jesus' name, so be it.

References to Scripture: Psalm 30:11; James 1:17; 1 Timothy 6:17

Prayer #12: When Your Child Is Far from Home

Lord, You see the pages in my sister's heart where her child lived, played, and grew. Now the daughter is gone from her embrace, and my friend struggles to trust You with her. Please dip Your pen into Your well of endless love, and write love letters of grace across her heart today. Give her words meant only for her, filling the pages of her soul with the sweet poetry of peace.

The empty pages waiting in hope have yellowed, curled, and all but turned to despair. Write a new story for my friend, a story of Your commitment to her child's well-being and peace. Whisper words of safety, fulfillment, and dreams realized. Show her Your plan to rescue her child from the schemes of the enemy. Let her clearly see her beloved child at Your feet and before Your throne, following You.

If my friend is tempted to obsess over lost opportunities, give her hope that You've not written the last chapter in her child's life yet. Reassure her that You have many people who can relate Your kindness and love into her daughter's heart. Bring those people to her, please, Father. You know the very ones she'll listen to. Protect her from wrong influences and deceptive voices.

Please fill up my friend's heart in ways that mean the most to her, whether a special song on the radio, a flower in bloom, or a call from a dear friend. You are the master of custom-made favors. Give my friend the ones she needs today, to keep her hopes focused on You.

And bring her child back home—home to her and home to You

In Jesus' name, so be it.

References to Scripture: Jeremiah 29:11; Ephesians 6:16; Isaiah 30:18

Prayer #13: When You Are Too Busy

Lord, my friend is choking on responsibilities. She is trying to do too much, to be all things to all people. I know this is not Your plan for her.

Because she loves people and fears disappointing them, she says yes more than she says no. Her schedule is crammed to bursting. Because she accomplishes tasks with excellence, she's a magnet to people who need things done.

And all this responsibility is causing her light to dim.

She was once so bright and eager to spend time with You, study Your life, tell others about Your love. Then she started working for You. And working. And working. The Devil knew he couldn't tempt her with robbing jewelry stores or murdering her neighbors, so he dangled the fruit of the business of the Lord in front of her. He convinced her that to be a worthy Christian, she had to stay busy, and that to say no was unholy.

Silence his lies to her, Lord. Woo her back to the place of rest and sweet contentment in Your presence, where the beam of Your smile is enough. Return the light to her eyes and the spring to her step.

Please help her find the balance You lived in when You walked on earth. You knew when to say "Okay, I'll do that," and when to say "Not interested," without worrying what others might think of You. You were secure in the Father's plan for You, not needing to please others in order to feel that Your light was bright enough.

Teach my friend Your ways, dear Lord. She doesn't want to burn out; she wants to sparkle and blaze with Your life, to do only those things You've called her to do. Then, when You come to take her home, she'll shine in heaven with You.

In Jesus' name, so be it.

References to Scripture: Jeremiah 29:11, John 6:38

Prayer #14: When Your Finances Are Not Enough

Lord, I love how You show Your extravagance in nature by placing an overabundance of seeds in every plant and tree to ensure they'll reproduce and nourish. You are *El Shaddai*, the God Who supplies and satisfies. My friend needs to see that side of You today.

She knows You as Lord and Savior, but to think of You as provider of material needs is unimaginable to her. Please reveal through Your Word that You aren't interested only in cleansing her spirit and renewing her soul. You also care about providing for her physical needs. I know this is true, because Jesus multiplied food for a crowd, healed bodies, and helped the poor. He lived a lifestyle of giving. And He hasn't changed.

In Jesus' name, I break the power of any lies Satan has told her about You not wanting her to go forward. I ask You to send truth that will set her free from erroneous ideas about You caring only for needs but never desires. Show her how lavish You can be, not for human greed or lust, but so we can help others and prove Your goodness.

Whatever seeds have grown this plant of a poverty mindset or poor money management, I ask You to uproot and replace with a new plant. So that she can prosper, teach my friend how to bear the fruit of wisdom, discipline, self-control, and a spirit of giving to others in need.

As she learns to trust that You are a giving God, please show her new avenues of income. Open her mind to ideas and ways of earning she's not considered before. Make her finances grow to the place where she is helping others learn Your secrets of success.

In Jesus' name, so be it.

References to Scripture: Genesis 17:1–2; Genesis 28:3; John 6:1–13; 21–43; John 13:29; Hebrews 13:8; John 8:31– 32; Psalm 37:4; Galatians 5:22–23; 3 John 2

Prayer #15: When You Think You Can't Forgive

Lord, You of all people know the depth of pain suffered from horrible wrongs that one doesn't deserve. So, You understand like no other the pain my friend feels today. This pain keeps her awake at night. It hounds her as she works, it claws and clutches at her gut, and it buzzes in her brain. The pain she feels might be for herself—for verbal or physical slaps and bruises—or for the scars that someone she loves is bearing.

She wants to forgive, to rip the irons of dark deeds and cutting words from her mind. But her soul lies in the dust of her offender, broken to ruins. She feels that forgiveness is beyond the capability of her broken soul.

This is where You come in.

Lord, I need You to bathe my friend's wounds and scars in the oil of Your mercy. Hold her heart in Your gentle hands— hands that create, heal, resurrect. Splash Your smile of acceptance and favor on her bent-over soul so she will feel Your pleasure that she is part of Your family and believe the love You have for her.

Take her to Your cross, Lord, as You hung naked, punished for crimes You didn't commit, paying for her sins and her abuser's wrongs against her. You rasped your forgiveness with a parched voice as You hung in shame, the Man Who never broke a law, taking death for us—people who break every one of your laws, along with Your heart. Yet You forgave and forgive, and You will again.

Give her a glimpse into the anguish that caused her enemy to hurt her. Let her see how weak and insecure he must be to rend the heart of another. Grant her mercy for the undeserved pain he inflicted, for the abuses that caused him to protect his scars with hate.

Then pick her up from the dust caked with Your blood, and hold her head high as she looks the abusive one in the eyes and tells him, "I forgive you, for Jesus' sake. When you hurt me, you really sinned against Him, my Maker. May He have compassion on us both."

In Jesus' name, so be it.

References to Scripture: 1 John 4:16; Luke 23:34; Colossians 3:13

Prayer #16: When a Loved One Has Passed Away

Alone. Hollow. Broken beyond repair. This is how my friend feels, Lord, since she said goodbye to her dear one. When strangers eased his body into the ground and covered it with earth, her heart sank with him. She knew her life would never be the same.

She wonders if she'll have the strength to face another sunrise. Her soul is all winter, with no hope or desire for spring. How can birds build nests and tulips bloom when her love lies buried? The enemy has convinced her that she's forgotten how to sing.

Yet You do not forget my friend, Your child. In the stillness of the night, when she reaches for phantom arms, You hold her. When morning reminds her that she must walk through another day without her loved one, You help her breathe. After the mailbox is empty of cards and the phone is silent, You sit with her, just being. Just loving.

Now more than ever, she needs Your friendship. She's known You as Lord, Master, and Savior. But today she craves companionship to sweeten her bitter cup. And You are the only One Whose sweet water can fill her emptiness.

God of all comfort, sing Your songs of mighty peace to my friend's heart. Awaken her to the glory of Your embrace.

Reveal to her new reasons to keep living, and new seasons of fruitfulness.

Send her companions whom You've chosen, not to take her loved one's place, but to color in the gray spots with fresh hues of gladness. Soft shades at first, as she opens the prison door of pain, and allows herself a glimpse of light, then brighter and bolder colors as she dares to step outside the door and bask in Your affection.

You alone can turn her sorrow into joy in ways none of us can imagine. Do what You do best, dear Lord: redeem this death, and from it, birth abundant life.

In Jesus' name, so be it.

References to Scripture: Isaiah 38:14; 2 Corinthians 1:3–4; Ephesians 2:14; John 14:27; Job 35:10; John 16:20; 1 Thessalonians 4:13–14; Revelation 21:4–5; John 10:10

Prayer #17: When You Face a Medical Test or Surgery

Lord, I know You love my friend worlds more than I can dream or imagine. Because of that conviction, I place her in Your hands as she goes through this medical test or surgery. Please let her feel Your presence and give her the assurance that You are with her and in her.

Help her to relax in Your embrace, dear Shepherd. Fill her mind with whatever scenes will calm her most. I bind the spirit of fear and anguish, in Jesus' name, from taking hold of her mind.

Guide the hands of the technicians, doctors, and nurses, Father. Give them a full night's sleep the night before, and nourishing meals leading up to the test or surgery. Keep them from strife with their family members and coworkers, please. Fill their minds with Your supernatural wisdom to know what not to do, what to do, and how to do it. I trust You to bring the most qualified people to help my friend.

I ask that any results from this test or surgery be clear so the doctors will know which treatment is best. If there is something that requires removal from my friend's body, I pray it comes out easily and completely, with no harm to adjoining organs or tissue.

May her recovery be swift and complete, with no recurring illness. Teach her how to take care of the wonderful temple You've given her so she stays healthy and strong, please.

Father, You knit my friend's body together when she was in the womb, and You know what it's going to take to fix her. Use this test or surgery as a means of healing her, as well as an experience of Your grace in her life. Let every person in the medical facility know that You are real and You alone are God. And may You receive glory from my friend's body, as she offers it to You as a living sacrifice.

In Jesus' name, so be it.

References to Scripture: Matthew 28:20; Matthew 18:18; 1 Corinthians 6:19; Psalm 139:15

Prayer #18: When You Need Special Wisdom to Raise Your Children

When my friend asked You for children, You did not disappoint her. You gave her the desire of her heart. Yet she longs for a deeper experience as a godly mother.

Some days all she manages to accomplish is doing laundry, preparing meals, and ensuring clean bodies. She longs for more time and energy to nurture her little ones in Your ways, training them to love and follow You. Please give her snippets of time when she can slip in a word, a song, or a prayer to show them You more clearly. Open her eyes to opportunities to offer her children the food of Your spirit and the water of life from Your throne.

When You held the children on Your lap and blessed them, I believe each one received a different word from You, according to their individual needs. Although every child is equally precious to You, no two have identical personalities. Your plan for each is custom-made. Please imprint that plan on my friend's heart as she raises her children, all so different in the way You formed them.

Give her supernatural grace to say no when they want to hear yes, and wisdom to say yes when no would damage their souls. Fill her with Your strong love that overcomes every fear. Grant her discernment of lies and of attempts to manipulate

Your good plan to childish ends. Teach her Your ways of discipline that lead to joyful obedience.

Keep her from condemnation when she falters and grief when she fails. Brighten her heart with contentment at each stage of her children's lives so she can enjoy them as You enjoy each lamb in Your flock.

May they rise and call her blessed. May she feel Your pleasure in the richness of her days as she fulfills the most important call You will ever place on her, the call to mother a child.

In Jesus' name, so be it.

References to Scripture: Psalm 37:4; Proverbs 22:6; Psalm 139; 15–16; 1 John 4:18; Hebrews 12:11; Romans 8:1–2; Proverbs 31:28

Prayer #19: When Anger Fills Your Soul

My friend has been wronged, Lord, and she's angry.

She knows that she's clutching this anger, Lord. Like a clothespin swells from the rain, then bakes dry and hard in the sun and clings to a garment to keep it on the line, her heart hangs onto her anger. And it's killing her. It's petrifying her soul, hardening it, keeping it from Your favor and affection.

Jesus, blow Your winds of life and love over her soul. Show her the times she has hurt You, and You chose to forgive instead of embracing the grief of a broken heart. You knew she'd do it again, yet You offered her Your grace.

By Your example, You teach us that when we are hurt, we must choose to forgive. You show us how to forgive, even when the same people hurt us over and over. Your love flowing through us empowers us to do so. Because You help us love ourselves and those around us, we're able to overcome stupid remarks or mean attitudes that try to keep us from the Father's grace-filled light. You teach us how to kill our bitterness with a decision.

Now, grace my friend to do that. Give her the life-giving power to kill this anger choking her freedom, her life, her joy. Get her off this clothesline where she's a prisoner, hanging on to the garment of hate. Teach her how to forgive, how to let go.

Reveal to her how You do it with us, every day and every minute.

Fill the empty places in her soul with the warmth of Your embrace, the light of Your presence, so You will be enough for her. And teach her how to live out of Your heart of mercy, so the grace to forgive is ready, even before she needs it.

In Jesus' name, so be it.

References to Scripture: Psalm 86:5; 1 John 1:9; 1 John 2:12; Mark 11:25–26

Prayer #20: When Someone Refuses
to Forgive You

Lord, You told us how many times we must forgive the same wrong someone inflicts on us. But You didn't say how many times we should ask for forgiveness and show we've repented before we give up trying to offer peace.

My friend knows she shouldn't have acted in an unloving way to her brother. And she's asked his forgiveness, even walked the second mile dozens of times to prove that she has changed her behavior. But he's shut her out of his life. He refuses to grant her even a slice of grace. He acts as if it pains him to say hello to her or be in the same room with her.

If her heart is bowed down in what she thinks is humility but is false guilt instead, teach her from Your spirit the true meaning of grace. Settle her confidence concerning her identity as Your child, loved and accepted in the Beloved. May her kindness extended to him flow from a loving heart, not guilt. Forever remove any leftovers of condemnation she feels from her wrong.

Give her ideas of how to pray for and bless him that no amount of defensiveness can conquer. Show her what measures of love her brother will best respond to, which will soften his heart the most. Do this not simply so she can know and feel his forgiveness, but also so he can receive forgiveness from You and live in freedom. For when we withhold grace, we use judgment as a wall to keep out conviction.

Perhaps he's refusing to forgive my friend so that he can prevent You from sneaking up on his heart. If so, take him by surprise, Lord, through my friend. Use the light in her heart to draw him to the light in You so they can worship at Your throne of grace together.

In Jesus' name, so be it.

References to Scripture: Matthew 18:22; Ephesians 1:6; Romans 8:1–2; Ephesians 4:3

Prayer #21: When You Need Physical Healing

Father, we know that Jesus was Your will personified on the earth, that He acted only upon what He saw You do and as You directed Him. Because He went about doing good and healing all who came to Him, I believe it is Your will to heal, and that You have not quit healing those who come to You in His name.

My sister is sick in her body and needs the healing that only You can give. We need divine intervention, the kind of stretching forth of Your hand of grace that You delight in, the kind that brings glory to Your name and seekers to Your feet.

Re-create what is broken or malfunctioning in my friend, please Lord. Restore her to the original design You intended when You knit her in her mother's womb and when You planned every good day for her before the world came into being, before sin scarred us with maladies.

If sin has snuck into a corner of her heart and conceals itself there, shine Your brightest sun to illumine every hidden snake clothed in dove's garments. Grant her repentance and joyful obedience so she can once again dance in Your embrace, free of hidden guilt.

Strengthen her faith in her inner being, where she rests deep in Your love, where she *knows* beyond her understanding that You want her well, that You are against disease and pain.

Help her reach out to You and believe that You not only *can* heal her, but that You also *want* to heal her. Yes, her. For she is precious to You.

May she not die but live to tell of Your mighty works. May her health be a salt bowl, causing others to thirst for the water of life that is You—always creating, giving, loving, healing.

In Jesus' name, so be it.

References to Scripture: John 5:19; Acts 10:38; John 9:3; Psalm 139:15–16; Jeremiah 29:11; Ephesians 3:16–17; Psalm 118:17

Prayer #22: When You Need Emotional Healing

My friend is tired down to her gut, Lord. She's tired of pretending she's okay when she wants to scream and weep and sink into the earth and never hurt again. You know how she feels, for You felt that same screaming ball of nothingness in Your belly as they draped You onto two wooden beams, then nailed You fast so You wouldn't escape the pain. A pain not only physical, but also the vilest soul pain at being separated from Your Father's heart that had embraced You and His voice that had guided You.

He turned His back on You, and You bore it so we wouldn't need to. Yet, she bears it anyway; broken and not knowing she can be whole, void of the hope for even a scrap of a put-together life.

Jesus, Shepherd Who never leaves a sheep alone, hold her until the hurt disappears. Tell her she's not a disappointment to You. Sing her songs You composed only for her and no other so she'll feel Your custom-made love and know You had a reason for creating her. Show her that reason in a thousand ways, dear Mender of Broken Lives.

She knows she's broken, but she doesn't know why, or she doesn't want to know for fear the pain is all her fault. Set her free with the truth that the thief has stolen her joy and ripped her value away. Shine the light of Your admiration for her into the deep places she's not aware of so she'll believe and not argue when You say, "I love you, daughter."

Grace her to release offenses she's held tightly in her fists and locked in the oldest diaries of her memory. Cause her to walk upright, gazing into Your broad smile of forgiveness and strength. Guide her steps to sweetest life. Make her believe that as she rests in the crook of Your arm and listens to Your lullabies, she can be whole.

In Jesus' name, so be it.

References to Scripture: Matthew 27:46; John 10:11–17; Psalm 139; John 10:10; 1 John 4:18

Prayer #23: When Your Plans Fall Through

Lord, my friend's plans were like a towering tree that branched to the heavens, its leaves bright with promise of shade for everyone she knew and some she didn't know, a glory for You and a joy for her. She believed the roots were formed in the soil of Your heart, of Your vision for her.

She watered her plans with worship to You for all the loveliness this tree would hold. She danced round the trunk as it grew and formed its stately shape. All who loved her rejoiced that it grew stronger and lovelier each year. As its fruit ripened and plumped, many partook of its sweet nourishment.

And now, its branches stare up at her, barren and twisted; its trunk a hollow shell where once a heart had beaten. Her vision is dead, her plans rotted and failed.

Lord, Your thoughts are only good for all Your children. Did my sister miss Your voice? Did she plant her own dreams, mistaking them for Yours? Afraid to blame herself, she's tempted to blame You. Confusion hounds her soul like branches pounding on windows in an angry storm.

Will You please take her shattered aspirations, the splintered wood from fallen trees, and replace them with truer, straighter saplings from Your heart, dear Grower of perfect plans. Rain the gift of living water upon this new dream, born not of her design, but of Your holy purpose.

Or, if it's Your will, resurrect her ruined plans, speaking life to the dead, proving You are mightier than death itself. You are life.

Whichever You choose, her times are in Your hand. Show Yourself strong on her behalf so she can dare to dream again, plan Your plans with You, and grow the tree of Your design. Give her hope for her future, a hope that's rooted and grounded in Your love.

In Jesus' name, so be it.

References to Scripture: Jeremiah 29:11; Psalm 31:15; John 11:25; Psalm 89:8

Prayer #24: When You Are Lonely

Lord, I know You see my friend's tears on her pillow, mingled with her bath water, and dripping onto her lap as she watches happy couples and families. Please capture her tears in Your bottle so they are not wasted in pity.

She is lonely, remembering the companion of her youth and maybe even longing to find a new soul mate. She fills her days and moments with craving attention, yet running from true affection. She's believed the lie that she is complete only if another shares her home and bed.

Yet because she is Your child, You have made her complete in You, with nothing missing or broken. She's bone of Your bone and flesh of Your flesh, Your child in whom You delight.

Visit her today, dear Lord and friend of the friendless. You know the brutal pain of being misunderstood by relatives, and you also suffered rejection from Your disciples. Show my friend the wounds in her heart that she hides behind so no one will see her pain. Bathe those wounds with the oil of Your Spirit. Bring healing from abuses and faithfulness in place of abandonment.

Open her eyes to see that You are more real than any human could be. Give her a longing to know You and seek Your companionship. Remove her fear of intimacy, of brokenness, of transparency. Show her how You see her, as Your princess seated with You, made to rule and reign.

Lead her to true friends—people who will love and nurture her in kind humility, not for their own use or gain. Protect her from evil companions, false friends, and a life filled with vanities. Bring her people she can befriend and help to grow so she doesn't become self-absorbed.

Please wipe the tears from her pillow and cradle her heart in Your tender hand until she finds her place of fulfillment in the center of Your heart.

In Jesus' name, so be it.

References to Scripture: Psalm 56:8; Colossians 2:10; Genesis 2:23; Revelation 21:9; Ephesians 2:6

Prayer #25: When a Loved One Is Mistreated

My friend watches, helpless, while one she loves is being mistreated. And that brand of pain cuts deeper than the abuses we suffer ourselves; it doubles our grief. You have experienced this twofold wounding, dear Father. You know how it feels to witness the Son of Your heart suffer from lies, bullying, and twisted words meant to bring ruin. You watched it all and loved Him through it, and finally You rescued Him—and Yourself—from the horror.

Do the same for my sister. Rescue her from the threat of bitterness and hate toward those who abuse her dear one. Soften her heart to bring them in prayer to Your throne of grace and mercy, for they need Your whispers of kindness. They walk in darkness and flail at the light. They are not fully aware of the consequences of their actions against this precious one You love.

Give her deep measures of Your power to forgive, to relinquish judgment to Your heart of truth. Only You know the anguish that causes bullies and abusers to bend to voices of evil and torment weaker ones. Only You can measure a heart against Your own and bring perfect justice.

Show my friend how best to pray for the wounding ones—and the wounded. Give her songs to sing over them, songs of deliverance and light. Guide her petitions with Your infinite wisdom. Cause her to prophesy truth into their lives so they can break free of Satan's afflictions.

Set her own heart free to worship You through her tears so Your presence will cover her. Give her relief in the night places as Your love cradles her heart in Yours. Cause her to dance in Your joyous embrace once again.

Allow her to witness the deliverance of her loved one, stronger and forever free. Use her story as a testimony of Your love and mercy.

In Jesus' name, so be it.

References to Scripture: Luke 23:34; Isaiah 30:18; Job 35:10; Ephesians 2:4

To you, beloved seeker of a Touchable God:

Thank you for taking time to read Touchable God. I pray your heart is encouraged by these stories and prayers, and that through them you've gained a clearer view of the Lord's immeasurable affection and concern for you.

I love connecting with readers! You can reach me in the following ways:

Hope Splashes, my website and blog: www.jeanettelevellie.com

Facebook: https://www.facebook.com/JeanetteLevellie

Goodreads: https://www.goodreads.com/author/dashboard

Pinterest: https://www.pinterest.com/jenlevellie/

Amazon Author Central: http://amzn.to/1TisY7w

Twitter: https://twitter.com/#!/JenLevellie

With grace and gratitude,

Jeanette Levellie